PRINCEWILL LAGANG

Finding Your One: A Christian Guide to Love

First published by PRINCEWILL LAGANG 2023

Copyright © 2023 by Princewill Lagang

All rights reserved. No part of this publication may be reproduced, stored or transmitted in any form or by any means, electronic, mechanical, photocopying, recording, scanning, or otherwise without written permission from the publisher. It is illegal to copy this book, post it to a website, or distribute it by any other means without permission.

Princewill Lagang asserts the moral right to be identified as the author of this work.

First edition

This book was professionally typeset on Reedsy.
Find out more at reedsy.com

Contents

1	The Quest for Love	1
2	The Foundations of Love	4
3	Preparing Your Heart and Mind	7
4	Meeting Potential Partners	10
5	Nurturing a Faith-Based Love Connection	13
6	The Power of Commitment	16
7	From Courtship to Covenant: Celebrating God-Ordained Love	19
8	Embracing God's Love Story	22
9	A Love that Endures	25
10	Love that Endures - A Comprehensive Guide	28
11	Love that Radiates	32
12	Embracing a Love that Transcends	35

1

The Quest for Love

In the Beginning

The sun hung low in the sky, casting a warm, golden glow over the small town of Graceville. A gentle breeze rustled the leaves of the ancient oak tree standing tall in the center of the town square. Birds sang their melodious tunes as the townsfolk went about their day. It was in this idyllic setting that Sarah found herself on the cusp of a journey, one that would lead her to discover the profound and transformative power of love.

Sarah had grown up in Graceville, a place where everyone knew their neighbors, and faith was the cornerstone of daily life. As a devout Christian, she had always believed in the sanctity of love, the kind of love that was deep, enduring, and divinely ordained. She was ready to embark on a quest to find her "one" – the person who would become her life partner, her soulmate, and her lifelong companion.

The Yearning Heart

For as long as she could remember, Sarah had felt a yearning deep within her heart. It was a desire to experience a love that transcended the superficial and fleeting emotions of the world. She longed for a love that was rooted in faith and guided by the principles she had learned from the Scriptures. Sarah believed that God had a plan for her life, including the person she was destined to be with, and she was determined to seek that divine plan.

In the early morning hours, as the first rays of sunlight broke through her bedroom window, Sarah would kneel in prayer, asking for guidance and strength on her quest for true love. She felt a profound connection to the verse in 1 Corinthians 13:4-7, which she had committed to memory:

"Love is patient, love is kind. It does not envy, it does not boast, it is not proud. It does not dishonor others, it is not self-seeking, it is not easily angered, it keeps no record of wrongs. Love does not delight in evil but rejoices with the truth. It always protects, always trusts, always hopes, always perseveres."

The Foundation of Faith

Sarah's journey was grounded in her unwavering faith. She believed that love was not just an emotion but a commitment, a covenant, and a reflection of God's love for His people. As she set out on her quest to find her "one," she knew she needed to approach this search with her faith at the forefront.

Sarah's faith community played a pivotal role in her life. The church was not just a place of worship but a source of guidance, support, and a community of like-minded believers. With the wisdom of her pastor and the counsel of her fellow churchgoers, Sarah felt equipped to navigate the path to finding her one true love.

Conclusion

The town of Graceville may have seemed like an ordinary place to an outsider, but to Sarah, it was the backdrop for a remarkable journey. In her quest to find love, she was determined to follow her faith, remain patient, and let God's divine plan unfold.

As we accompany Sarah on her journey in this book, we will explore the profound principles and teachings that can guide us in our own pursuit of love as Christians. Love, as the Bible teaches, is the greatest of virtues, and the journey to find "the one" can be a transformative and sacred experience. In the chapters to come, we will delve into the values, actions, and reflections that can lead us to the love we seek, the love God intended for us to find.

Join us in exploring the Christian path to love, as we embark on a journey to uncover the meaning of true, lasting, and God-given love.

2

The Foundations of Love

Building on the Rock

Sarah knew that finding her one true love required a strong foundation. Just as a house built on a solid rock withstands storms, a love relationship rooted in faith and purpose can weather the trials of life. In this chapter, we'll explore the foundational principles that underpin the Christian journey to love.

Faith: The Cornerstone

The cornerstone of Christian love is faith, both in God and in the love that God has planned for each individual. Faith is not just a belief in something unseen but a deep trust in God's divine plan for our lives. Sarah often found solace in Hebrews 11:1, which says, "Now faith is confidence in what we hope for and assurance about what we do not see." Trusting in God's timing and wisdom is vital in the search for true love.

Love Thyself: Self-Worth and Respect

Before seeking love from others, it's crucial to love and respect oneself as a child of God. The Bible teaches in Matthew 22:39, "Love your neighbor as yourself." This verse reminds us that self-love is a prerequisite for loving others. By recognizing one's own worth and nurturing self-esteem, we become better equipped to enter into healthy, loving relationships.

Agape Love: Unconditional and Selfless Love

Christian love is often described as "agape" love, a selfless, sacrificial love that seeks the well-being of others. This love mirrors God's love for us, and as we explore love relationships, striving for agape love is the ultimate goal. Sarah kept 1 Corinthians 13:4-7 in her heart as a reminder of what agape love should look like. It is patient, kind, forgiving, and unwavering in its commitment.

Understanding Compatibility: Faith and Values

In the search for love, compatibility is not solely based on shared interests or physical attraction but on a shared foundation of faith and values. Sarah believed that when two people align their faith and values, they can build a strong and lasting love together. This alignment is what makes a relationship thrive even in times of adversity.

Patience and God's Timing

Patience is a virtue, especially in the journey to find your one true love. Ecclesiastes 3:1 tells us, "There is a time for everything, and a season for every activity under the heavens." Trusting in God's timing can help individuals remain patient and avoid rushing into relationships that may not align with His plan.

Community Support: The Role of Friends and Family

The love journey doesn't happen in isolation. Friends and family play a crucial role in providing advice, guidance, and support. Proverbs 11:14 says, "Where there is no guidance, a people falls, but in an abundance of counselors, there is safety." Seek counsel from those who share your values and faith, as they can offer valuable insights.

Conclusion

The journey to find your one true love in a Christian context is about building a strong foundation on faith, self-worth, agape love, shared values, patience, and community support. These foundational principles will guide us as we navigate the complexities of love relationships in the chapters to come.

In the next chapter, we will delve into the practical aspects of how to begin the search for love while staying true to your Christian faith. Whether you are single or in a relationship, understanding how to apply these principles in your daily life is crucial on the path to finding your one.

3

Preparing Your Heart and Mind

The Search Begins

Sarah was now ready to embark on her journey to find her one true love. But before she could begin actively seeking a life partner, she knew it was essential to prepare her heart and mind. In this chapter, we'll explore the initial steps on this exciting path.

Self-Reflection: Know Thyself

The first step in preparing your heart and mind for love is to engage in deep self-reflection. Take time to understand who you are, your values, and your life goals. Psalm 139:14 reminds us that we are "fearfully and wonderfully made" by God. Embrace your uniqueness and understand how it can shape your relationship.

Define Your Relationship Goals

What are your relationship goals and what kind of love are you seeking? Sarah had a clear vision of the love she wanted, one grounded in faith and agape love. Defining your relationship goals will help you recognize the right person when they come into your life.

Prayer: Seek Guidance from God

Just as Sarah started each day with prayer, seeking guidance from God is a crucial part of preparing for love. Pour out your heart to God, share your desires, and ask for His guidance and wisdom in your journey. Proverbs 3:5-6 encourages us to "trust in the Lord with all your heart and lean not on your understanding."

Let Go of Past Baggage

Before you can fully embrace a new love, it's essential to let go of any past hurts, grudges, or emotional baggage that might hinder your future relationships. Forgiveness and healing are vital to open your heart to new love. Colossians 3:13 advises, "Bear with each other and forgive one another if any of you has a grievance against someone."

Stay Committed to Your Faith

As you prepare your heart and mind for love, maintain a strong commitment to your faith. Your relationship with God is the foundation of your journey, and by staying faithful to your beliefs, you ensure that any love that comes into your life aligns with your Christian values.

Cultivate a Supportive Community

Surround yourself with a supportive community of friends and family who understand and encourage your pursuit of Christian love. They can offer guidance and provide accountability to help you stay on track.

Conclusion

Preparing your heart and mind for love is a vital step in the journey to find your one true love. By engaging in self-reflection, defining your relationship goals, seeking guidance from God, letting go of past baggage, staying committed to your faith, and cultivating a supportive community, you set the stage for a love that is deep, meaningful, and rooted in your Christian values.

In the following chapter, we will delve into the practical steps for meeting potential partners while keeping your faith and values at the forefront of your search. As you prepare your heart and mind, remember that love is a divine gift, and when the time is right, it will be revealed to you by God's plan.

4

Meeting Potential Partners

The Path to Connection

With her heart and mind prepared, Sarah was now ready to meet potential partners in her journey to find true love. This chapter explores the practical steps you can take to connect with potential life partners while staying true to your Christian faith.

Engage in Christian Community

One of the most fruitful places to meet like-minded individuals who share your faith is within your Christian community. Attend church events, Bible studies, and volunteer activities. It's in these settings that you're more likely to meet people who prioritize faith and values in their lives.

Online Dating: A Modern Approach

In the digital age, online dating can be a practical way to meet potential partners who align with your values. When using online platforms, it's crucial to choose Christian-specific dating sites that cater to individuals who prioritize faith in their relationships. Maintain honesty and transparency in your online interactions, and make your intentions clear from the outset.

Join Interest-Based Groups

Engage in activities or groups that align with your interests and values. Whether it's a Christian book club, a volunteer organization, or a sports league, participating in such groups can naturally lead to connections with like-minded individuals.

Friendships: A Solid Foundation

Many lasting relationships begin as friendships. Building a strong foundation of friendship can help you get to know someone on a deeper level before moving into a romantic relationship. Proverbs 18:24 tells us that "a man of many companions may come to ruin, but there is a friend who sticks closer than a brother."

Evaluate Potential Partners

As you meet potential partners, evaluate their compatibility with your values and relationship goals. Engage in meaningful conversations about faith, values, and life goals. Don't rush into a romantic relationship without first assessing whether the person aligns with your vision of a Christian love relationship.

Prayer and Discernment

Continuing to seek God's guidance is essential during this phase. Pray for discernment to recognize if the individuals you meet are in alignment with God's plan for your life. Trust that God will guide you toward the right person.

Community Support and Accountability

Maintain a support system of friends and family who can provide guidance and accountability. Share your experiences and thoughts with them, and welcome their insights and advice.

Conclusion

Meeting potential partners is a significant step on your journey to finding your one true love as a Christian. Engaging in your Christian community, exploring online dating thoughtfully, joining interest-based groups, building friendships, evaluating compatibility, seeking God's guidance, and relying on community support will help you navigate this phase.

In the upcoming chapter, we'll delve into the process of nurturing a loving relationship once you've found a potential life partner. This chapter will explore the essential aspects of building a strong, enduring, and faith-based love connection.

5

Nurturing a Faith-Based Love Connection

The Beginning of a Beautiful Journey

As Sarah met someone who shared her faith, values, and vision for a Christian love relationship, she knew that the journey to finding her one was entering a new phase. This chapter explores the steps to nurturing a faith-based love connection that can stand the test of time.

Communication: The Key to Understanding

Open and honest communication is the cornerstone of any healthy relationship. In your faith-based love journey, take time to share your thoughts, feelings, and beliefs with your partner. Proverbs 27:9 reminds us, "Oil and perfume make the heart glad, and the sweetness of a friend comes from his earnest counsel." Share your thoughts earnestly and listen to your partner's counsel.

Shared Spiritual Growth

One of the joys of a faith-based relationship is the opportunity for shared spiritual growth. Engage in activities such as Bible study, prayer, and attending church together. These shared experiences can deepen your connection and faith.

Prayer as a Couple

Prayer is a powerful tool to strengthen your relationship. Take time to pray together, seeking God's guidance, and asking for His blessings on your journey as a couple. Matthew 18:20 reminds us, "For where two or three are gathered in my name, there am I among them."

Conflict Resolution: A Test of Faith

In any relationship, conflicts may arise. In a faith-based love connection, it's vital to approach conflicts with patience, forgiveness, and the desire for resolution. Remember the words of Ephesians 4:32, "Be kind to one another, tenderhearted, forgiving one another, as God in Christ forgave you."

Trust and Accountability

Trust is the foundation of any relationship. Trust that your partner shares your faith and values and that they will respect and uphold them. Maintain accountability to each other and to God, knowing that your love is rooted in a divine purpose.

Preparing for the Future

In a faith-based love relationship, it's important to discuss your future together. Share your dreams, aspirations, and goals, ensuring they align with your shared values and faith. Seek God's guidance for your future as a couple.

Community Support

Just as your community supported you in earlier phases of your journey, continue to seek guidance and support from friends and family. They can provide valuable insights and encouragement.

Conclusion

Nurturing a faith-based love connection is an ongoing and deeply rewarding journey. Communication, shared spiritual growth, prayer, conflict resolution, trust, accountability, and planning for the future are all essential aspects of building a strong and enduring love connection.

In the next chapter, we'll explore the significance of commitment and what it means to fully commit to a faith-based love relationship. Understanding the nature of commitment is crucial to ensuring that your love remains strong and enduring.

6

The Power of Commitment

The Significance of Commitment

As Sarah's relationship with a like-minded Christian partner continued to grow, the importance of commitment became increasingly clear. This chapter delves into the profound role that commitment plays in a faith-based love relationship.

Understanding the Biblical Concept of Commitment

Commitment is a fundamental concept in Christianity. God's commitment to His people, as depicted throughout the Bible, serves as a model for human commitment. 2 Timothy 2:13 reminds us that "if we are faithless, he remains faithful, for he cannot disown himself." This unwavering commitment is a powerful example for Christian relationships.

Commitment as a Choice

In a faith-based love connection, commitment is not merely a feeling but a conscious choice. It is a decision to stand by your partner through all seasons of life, just as God stands by His people through every circumstance. Philippians 2:2 encourages us to "make my joy complete by being like-minded, having the same love, being one in spirit and of one mind." This unity is born out of commitment.

Weathering Life's Storms

Commitment is the anchor that keeps a relationship steady in the face of life's challenges. The storms of life may come in the form of health issues, financial struggles, or personal setbacks. A faith-based love relationship is tested in adversity, but a strong commitment ensures that you face these challenges together, as a team.

Faithfulness and Trust

Commitment and faithfulness go hand in hand. The Bible is clear in its emphasis on faithfulness, as seen in Galatians 5:22-23, which lists faithfulness as one of the fruits of the Spirit. Faithfulness and trust are mutually reinforcing, and they build a solid foundation for your love relationship.

The Covenant of Marriage

In a Christian love journey, the ultimate expression of commitment is marriage. Marriage is not just a legal or social contract; it's a sacred covenant before God. Ephesians 5:31 states, "For this reason, a man will leave his father and mother and be united to his wife, and the two will become one flesh." This unity signifies a profound commitment to love, honor, and cherish one another.

Community Accountability

Community support and accountability continue to be crucial throughout your love journey. Share your commitment to your partner with friends and family, and welcome their prayers and encouragement. Accountability to your community strengthens your commitment.

Conclusion

Commitment is the binding force that ensures the longevity and strength of a faith-based love relationship. In the next chapter, we will explore the final phase of the love journey: the culmination of a Christian love relationship in marriage and the celebration of the love that God has orchestrated. Understanding the significance of this phase will help you fully appreciate the beauty of a faith-based love story.

7

From Courtship to Covenant: Celebrating God-Ordained Love

The Culmination of Love

As Sarah's faith-based love journey progressed, she and her partner moved closer to the culmination of their relationship: marriage. This chapter explores the final phase of a Christian love relationship and the profound significance of celebrating God-ordained love.

The Covenant of Marriage: A Sacred Commitment

In the Christian faith, marriage is not just a legal or social contract; it is a sacred covenant before God. Genesis 2:24 tells us, "That is why a man leaves his father and mother and is united to his wife, and they become one flesh." In marriage, two individuals become one in spirit and purpose, and their commitment is blessed by God.

Preparing for Marriage

As you move toward marriage, it's crucial to engage in premarital preparation.

This can involve premarital counseling, discussions about future goals, and understanding the roles and responsibilities of a Christian marriage. Ephesians 5:25 emphasizes the role of husbands: "Husbands, love your wives, just as Christ loved the church and gave himself up for her." This love mirrors Christ's love for His people.

The Wedding Ceremony: A Divine Celebration

The wedding ceremony is not just a social event; it is a sacred celebration of the love that God has orchestrated. The presence of God and His blessings are invited into the marriage, signifying His central role in the relationship. The exchange of vows and the commitment made before God and witnesses make this moment profoundly meaningful.

The Role of Community: Support and Accountability

Throughout the marriage preparation and the wedding ceremony, your community plays a significant role. They offer support, encouragement, and accountability. Proverbs 15:22 reminds us, "Plans fail for lack of counsel, but with many advisers, they succeed." Seek guidance from those who have walked this path and share your joy with them.

Building a Strong Foundation: Love, Faith, and Trust

In the early days of marriage, focus on building a strong foundation of love, faith, and trust. Continue to pray together, engage in shared spiritual growth, and remain committed to open and honest communication. Ephesians 5:33 highlights the importance of mutual respect and love: "However, each one of you also must love his wife as he loves himself, and the wife must respect her husband."

Conclusion: Embracing God's Blessing

As you celebrate your faith-based love in marriage, remember that God's blessing is upon your union. Your love story, guided by faith and commitment, is a testament to the power of God-ordained love. By embracing God's blessing, you embark on a lifelong journey filled with love, joy, and a shared purpose that glorifies Him.

In the final chapter, we will reflect on the journey Sarah took, the love she found, and the wisdom she gained throughout her Christian guide to love. Her story serves as an inspiration for all who seek to find their one true love in the embrace of faith and the guidance of God.

8

Embracing God's Love Story

Reflecting on the Journey

As Sarah looked back on her Christian guide to love, she realized that her journey was a testament to the enduring power of faith and commitment. In this final chapter, we reflect on the wisdom and lessons learned from her experience and explore the broader context of embracing God's love story.

The Wisdom of Patience

Throughout her journey, Sarah learned the wisdom of patience. God's timing is perfect, and waiting for the right person, the "one," is worth it. Ecclesiastes 3:1 reminds us that "there is a time for everything, and a season for every activity under the heavens." Trusting in God's timing leads to beautiful outcomes.

The Beauty of Agape Love

Agape love, the selfless and sacrificial love that Sarah embraced, was the cornerstone of her relationship. It's a love that mirrors God's love for His people. As she experienced and demonstrated this love, she found that it was both powerful and transformative.

The Strength of Commitment

Commitment in a Christian love relationship is unwavering and resilient. It's the glue that holds the relationship together in the face of challenges. In Sarah's journey, commitment proved to be the key to a lasting and fulfilling love story.

The Role of Faith and Prayer

Faith and prayer were constants in Sarah's journey. She leaned on her faith to guide her decisions and sought God's wisdom through prayer. Her faith strengthened her relationship and provided her with guidance in times of uncertainty.

The Joy of Community Support

Sarah's story emphasized the importance of community support. Friends and family offered her encouragement, advice, and accountability. Proverbs 27:17 reminds us that "as iron sharpens iron, so one person sharpens another." This mutual support helped her stay true to her faith and values.

Celebrating God's Plan

In embracing God's love story, Sarah celebrated the divine plan that brought her and her partner together. Her relationship was a testament to the beauty of a love guided by faith, rooted in values, and celebrated through the covenant of marriage.

Continuing the Journey

Sarah's story is a beautiful example of the Christian guide to love. As you reflect on her journey, consider how the wisdom she gained can inspire your own love story. Remember that your journey, guided by faith, commitment, and the love of God, is unique and filled with purpose. Embrace your own love story, knowing that it is a part of God's divine plan.

In closing, we encourage you to seek God's guidance in your quest to find your one true love, following the principles of faith and commitment that Sarah's journey has illuminated. Your love story, too, can be a testament to the enduring and transformative power of God-ordained love.

9

A Love that Endures

The Journey Continues

As we continue our exploration of Sarah's Christian guide to love, we come to a chapter that celebrates the enduring nature of love. Love, especially the kind rooted in faith and commitment, has the capacity to weather the storms of life and shine even in the darkest of hours. In this chapter, we delve into the qualities and principles that allow love to endure.

Faith as an Anchor

Faith is the bedrock upon which enduring love is built. Just as a ship relies on its anchor to remain steady in a turbulent sea, faith acts as the anchor in a love relationship, holding it firm even when the world around may seem chaotic. Hebrews 11:1 reminds us that "faith is the substance of things hoped for, the evidence of things not seen." In love, this faith sustains hope and trust in a shared future, even in challenging times.

Perseverance in Times of Adversity

No relationship is without its trials and tribulations. Sarah's journey showed us that enduring love is not about avoiding adversity but about persevering through it. The ability to work through difficulties, communicate honestly, and seek resolution is the mark of a love that can endure any challenge.

Embracing Change and Growth

Love is not static; it evolves and grows over time. Just as individuals change, so do relationships. Embracing this change, and supporting each other's personal growth, is vital to a love that endures. As Sarah's story illustrated, the ability to adapt to life's changes while staying rooted in faith is a testament to the strength of enduring love.

The Power of Forgiveness

Forgiveness is a cornerstone of enduring love. In the face of mistakes and misunderstandings, the capacity to forgive and seek forgiveness is a healing balm for the relationship. Colossians 3:13 reminds us to "bear with each other and forgive one another if any of you has a grievance against someone." Forgiveness is a testament to the enduring nature of love.

Shared Goals and Dreams

In the journey of enduring love, shared goals and dreams are the compass that keeps the relationship on course. It's essential to regularly check in with your partner, discuss your aspirations, and ensure that your individual and collective dreams align.

The Gift of Time

Love that endures is patient and understands the value of time. Just as a tree grows stronger with each passing year, love deepens and becomes more resilient as it weathers the seasons of life. Ecclesiastes 3:1 reminds us that "there is a time for everything, and a season for every activity under the heavens." In love, understanding the importance of the right time and season is a hallmark of its enduring nature.

Conclusion

Enduring love, as Sarah's journey illuminated, is a profound gift that requires faith, perseverance, the ability to adapt and grow, the power of forgiveness, shared dreams, and the gift of time. As we conclude this chapter and reflect on the enduring nature of love, we are reminded that love, especially in a Christian context, is a beacon of hope and a testament to the divine plan for our lives.

In the final chapter, we will wrap up this guide to love, drawing on the wisdom and lessons learned from Sarah's journey to provide a comprehensive overview of how to seek, nurture, and sustain a love that endures.

10

Love that Endures - A Comprehensive Guide

Reflecting on the Journey

In this concluding chapter of "Finding Your One: A Christian Guide to Love," we bring together the wisdom and lessons from Sarah's journey. We've explored the search for love, the preparation of the heart and mind, the meeting of potential partners, the nurturing of a faith-based love connection, and the celebration of God-ordained love. Now, we create a comprehensive guide for seeking, nurturing, and sustaining love that truly endures.

Seeking Love

1. Grounded in Faith: Begin your journey with a firm foundation in your Christian faith. Trust in God's plan for your life and rely on His guidance.

2. Self-Reflection: Take time to know yourself, your values, and your relationship goals. Understand what you're looking for in a love relationship.

3. Define Your Relationship Goals: Clarify your vision of love and identify the qualities and values you seek in a partner.

4. Prayer and Patience: Start each day with prayer, seeking God's guidance and remaining patient as you wait for His timing.

Meeting Potential Partners

5. Christian Community: Engage in your Christian community, attending church events, Bible studies, and volunteer activities where you're likely to meet like-minded individuals.

6. Online Dating: Consider Christian-specific online dating platforms that cater to individuals who prioritize faith in their relationships.

7. Interest-Based Groups: Join groups and activities that align with your interests and values, as this can lead to natural connections with like-minded individuals.

8. Friendships First: Build strong foundations through friendships, getting to know potential partners on a deeper level before pursuing romance.

Nurturing a Faith-Based Love Connection

9. Open Communication: Maintain open and honest communication with your partner, sharing thoughts, feelings, and beliefs.

10. Shared Spiritual Growth: Engage in activities like Bible study, prayer, and attending church together to deepen your connection and faith.

11. Prayer as a Couple: Strengthen your relationship by praying together, seeking God's guidance, and inviting His presence.

12. Conflict Resolution and Trust: Approach conflicts with patience, forgiveness, and a commitment to resolution. Build trust in your relationship.

Commitment that Endures

13. The Biblical Concept of Commitment: Understand that commitment is a conscious choice, just as God remains faithful to His people.

14. Weathering Life's Storms: Expect and prepare for life's challenges, knowing that commitment will keep your relationship steady.

15. Faithfulness and Trust: Mutual faithfulness and trust are essential for a strong relationship foundation.

16. The Covenant of Marriage: Embrace the sacred commitment of marriage, and engage in premarital preparation to ensure a strong foundation.

Celebrating God-Ordained Love

17. The Wedding Ceremony: Celebrate your love in a sacred ceremony that invites God's blessings into your marriage.

18. Community Support: Continue to seek guidance and support from friends and family who understand the significance of your faith-based love.

Nurturing Love that Endures

19. Patience: Understand that God's timing is perfect, and waiting for the right person is worth it.

20. Agape Love: Embrace selfless, sacrificial love, and practice it in your relationship.

21. Strength of Commitment: Recognize commitment as unwavering and resilient, the glue that holds your relationship together.

22. Adversity and Perseverance: Persevere through challenges, knowing that enduring love is not about avoiding adversity but about working through it.

23. Embracing Change and Growth: Support each other's personal growth and adapt to the changes in your relationship.

24. The Power of Forgiveness: Forgive and seek forgiveness, offering healing in the face of mistakes and misunderstandings.

25. Shared Goals and Dreams: Continuously discuss your aspirations and ensure they align with your shared values and faith.

26. The Gift of Time: Understand the value of time and how love deepens as it weathers the seasons of life.

Embracing God's Love Story

As you wrap up this guide to love, remember that your love story is a part of God's divine plan. Embrace His guidance and blessings throughout your journey. Your faith-based love is a testament to the enduring and transformative power of love, and your story, like Sarah's, can inspire others in their pursuit of love that truly endures.

11

Love that Radiates

The Continuing Journey

In the previous chapter, we explored how to create a love that endures. Now, in Chapter 11 of "Finding Your One: A Christian Guide to Love," we delve into how your enduring love can radiate and impact not just your relationship but also the world around you.

The Influence of Radiant Love

Sarah's love story served as a powerful testimony to the transformative influence of love rooted in faith and commitment. Her love, which endured through time and adversity, radiated in a way that inspired and impacted those in her life.

Sharing Your Love Story

One way your love can radiate is by sharing your love story with others. Testify to the power of enduring love and the role of faith in your relationship. Encourage others on their journeys and let them see how God's plan for your life unfolded.

Community Impact

Consider how your love can impact your community. By nurturing a strong, faith-based relationship, you can serve as a model for others. Your love and commitment can inspire those around you, whether it's your church community, family, or friends.

Support and Counsel

Radiant love often comes from the support and counsel of those who have walked the path before you. Seek the wisdom of mentors and friends who can provide guidance and encouragement as you continue to strengthen your love.

Charity and Acts of Love

A love that radiates extends beyond your relationship. Engage in charity and acts of love, both as a couple and individually, to share your blessings and be a source of positivity in the world. Acts of love can include volunteering, supporting those in need, and being empathetic and kind to others.

Faith in Action

Let your faith be visible in your actions. Continue to pray as a couple, serve in your faith community, and live out your shared values. Your faith in action can be a powerful testament to the transformative potential of enduring love.

The Impact of Radiant Love

Radiant love is not just a source of inspiration for others; it can also have a profound impact on your own relationship. As you continue to share your love and values, you reinforce the principles that brought you together in the first place.

Conclusion

As you move forward on your journey of love that endures, remember the potential for your love to radiate and inspire others. Whether through sharing your story, impacting your community, supporting and counseling others, engaging in charity and acts of love, or putting your faith into action, your love can be a source of light in the world.

In the final chapter of this guide, we'll reflect on the overarching themes and wisdom you've gained throughout the journey, encouraging you to continue seeking, nurturing, and sharing a love that is deeply rooted in faith and commitment.

12

Embracing a Love that Transcends

The Journey's End and a New Beginning

In this concluding chapter of "Finding Your One: A Christian Guide to Love," we reflect on the transformative journey you've undertaken. Your path, guided by faith and commitment, has led you to a love that transcends the ordinary, and it's worth celebrating the lessons you've learned.

The Lessons of Love

Throughout this guide, we've explored the principles and values that underpin Christian love. From seeking love rooted in faith and commitment to nurturing a faith-based connection, celebrating God-ordained love, and creating a love that endures, you've acquired a wealth of wisdom.

Embracing God's Plan

Your love story is a testament to the divine plan for your life. As you've journeyed through each chapter, you've learned that God's timing is perfect, that faith is the anchor, that commitment is the glue, and that enduring love is possible.

Your Love Story

Now that you've discovered and nurtured a love that transcends, your love story can continue to inspire others. Your enduring love, rooted in faith, serves as a living testament to the power of God-ordained love. Your story can encourage others in their quests to find and nurture love that endures.

The Ongoing Journey

Your journey doesn't end with finding your one. It's a lifelong adventure that's filled with joy, challenges, growth, and faith. Continue to seek God's guidance, to pray together, and to be a source of inspiration and love in your community.

Embracing a Love that Transcends

A love that transcends is a love that goes beyond the everyday. It's a love that's guided by a higher purpose, bound by faith and commitment, and capable of withstanding the trials of life. Embrace this love and let it radiate in your relationship, your community, and the world.

Conclusion

As we conclude "Finding Your One: A Christian Guide to Love," take a moment to reflect on your journey. You've learned the importance of faith, commitment, patience, and perseverance. You've discovered the enduring power of love and how it can transform your life and inspire others.

Your love story is a unique chapter in God's divine plan, and it serves as a beacon of hope for those who seek love that is deeply rooted in faith and commitment. As you continue your journey, remember that your love story is an ongoing testament to the love that transcends the ordinary and reflects the boundless love of God.

Book Summary: Finding Your One - A Christian Guide to Love

"Finding Your One: A Christian Guide to Love" is a heartfelt and comprehensive journey through the quest for love that's deeply rooted in faith and commitment. This book follows the story of Sarah, a Christian seeking her one true love, as she navigates the complexities of modern relationships with a steadfast commitment to her Christian values.

Chapter 1: The Search Begins

The journey starts with Sarah's desire to find her life partner, emphasizing the importance of faith and patience in the search for the one.

Chapter 2: Preparing Your Heart and Mind

To find true love, one must begin by preparing their heart and mind. This chapter explores the importance of self-reflection, defining relationship goals, prayer, letting go of past baggage, and staying committed to one's faith.

Chapter 3: Meeting Potential Partners

This chapter provides practical advice on where and how to meet potential life partners, including engaging with the Christian community, utilizing online dating, joining interest-based groups, and building friendships.

Chapter 4: Nurturing a Faith-Based Love Connection

Once a potential partner is found, the focus shifts to nurturing the relationship. This chapter covers essential aspects such as open communication, shared spiritual growth, prayer as a couple, conflict resolution, trust, and accountability.

Chapter 5: The Power of Commitment

With the foundation of the relationship in place, the role of commitment is explored. Commitment, grounded in faith and the biblical concept, is vital in weathering life's storms and maintaining a strong, enduring relationship.

Chapter 6: From Courtship to Covenant: Celebrating God-Ordained Love

The culmination of a faith-based love relationship is marriage. This chapter delves into the significance of the covenant of marriage, premarital preparation, and the wedding ceremony as a celebration of God-ordained love.

Chapter 7: Love that Endures

This chapter emphasizes the enduring nature of love, discussing the qualities that allow love to weather challenges and evolve over time. It also highlights the power of faith, perseverance, adaptability, forgiveness, shared goals, and the value of time.

Chapter 8: Love that Radiates

Radiant love has the power to inspire and impact not only the relationship itself but also the world around. This chapter encourages sharing your love story, impacting your community, supporting and counseling others, engaging in acts of love, putting faith into action, and reinforcing the transformative potential of enduring love.

Chapter 9: Embracing a Love that Transcends

In the final chapter, the book reflects on the entire journey, highlighting the lessons learned, the importance of faith, and the power of a love story that transcends the ordinary. It encourages readers to continue seeking God's guidance and sharing their own inspiring love stories.

"Finding Your One: A Christian Guide to Love" offers valuable insights and guidance for those embarking on a journey to find love deeply rooted in faith and commitment. It's a testament to the enduring and transformative power of God-ordained love.

www.ingramcontent.com/pod-product-compliance
Lightning Source LLC
LaVergne TN
LVHW010439070526
838199LV00066B/6090